THE GIFT OF GOLF

Written by Venessa Fellin

Amazon Book Publishing Center
420 Terry Ave N, Seattle,
Washington, 98109, U.S.A

To my golf-loving husband and our little caddy Ava: Thanks for helping me pen my first book about the 'tee-rific' gift of golf. With your support, every page was a hole-in-one! Here's to swinging through life together on and off the green.

Love, Venessa

Once upon a time, in a sunny little town,
there lived a dad named Dave
who loved to swing it around.

With his trusty golf clubs
and a beautiful day

he would head to the course
ready to play.

Early in the morning,
when the grass was still dewy,
he would tee up
feeling oh so groovy.

He'd lineup his shot
with precision and care,
and off went the ball
so high in the air.

His swings were so graceful,
smooth, and so neat.

He aimed for the fairway where
the grass was so sweet.

Dad, can I join you?
His child would say
with eyes full of wonder,
ready to play.

Dad chuckles and smiles.
He couldn't resist

showing interest in golf
was a moment of bliss.

With every new stroke,
he would show him such fun
and the joys of golfing
under the sun.

They would head to the range
and hit balls for a while,
hitting side-by-side.
Dad could hit it a mile.

The little one swung
with all of his might,
giggling and laughing,
this day felt so right.

Dad taught him great patience
as he searched for the ball
in the tall grass
he would sometimes crawl.

He showed them good manners,
always polite,
teaching them lessons
to show them what's right.

They would line up their putts,
give them a roll,
and hit them so well that
they went right in the hole.

Dad cheered them on with each hole they'd complete, knowing that bonding was time spent so sweet.

Through the ups and the downs,
he would teach him life lessons.
The kid had such fun,
wanting more sessions.

?
90°

Dad's love for the game
and the joys it would bring
made him as happy
as the songbirds who sing

And so,
in this tale of dad golfing away,
we learn that
his kid also loves to go play.

Whether it's on the old course
or at home with the crew,
the bond that they share is
so strong and so true.
So next time you go with your dad to
play, look for these three
and make sure to say hey.

ABOUT THE AUTHOR

Venessa Fellin, an exciting new voice in children's literature, presents "The Gift of Golf," a heartwarming tale that captures the bond between a father and his children through the lens of golf. With a delightful blend of warmth and wonder, Venessa weaves a story that celebrates family, love, and the joy of sharing a beloved pastime. Through her enchanting narrative, young readers are invited to discover the magic of golf and the enduring connections it fosters within a family.

THE END

9 798889 324063 4